W9-AHW-859

For current pricing information,
or to learn more about this or any Nextext title,
call us toll-free at **1-800-323-5435**
or visit our web site at www.nextext.com.

RAY WILTSEY MIDDLE SCHOOL
1450 East G Street
Ontario, CA 91764

A CLASSIC RETELLING

The Call *of the* WILD

by Jack London

nextext

Printed in the United States of America
ISBN 0-618-00373-8

2 3 4 5 6 7 — QKT — 05 04 03 02 01

Table of Contents

The Gold Rush in Canada's Yukon creates a market for sled dogs. Buck is a smart dog, as well as being big and strong. A man who worked for his owner sells Buck to a stranger who makes Buck a sled dog. Buck feels angry and tries to attack a man, who beats him with a club. Buck learns never to disobey a man with a club. Two mail carriers named Perrault and François buy Buck to work their sled.

Buck soon learns the ways of the dogs. They all fight for food and for survival. He sees the dog named Curly killed by the pack for trying to make friends with a mean husky. As Curly begins to die, the other dogs pounce on her and eat her. Buck obeys the commands of the men out of fear of being whipped. The weather is cold, and there is never enough food. No longer living with people who love him, he listens to his own instincts and quickly becomes wild.

III: The Dominant Beast

Buck wants to replace Spitz as the lead dog. One cold night, Buck attacks Spitz. As they fight, a pack of starving wild dogs comes along, smelling blood and hoping to eat the loser. The sled dogs chase the wild dogs away and spend the night in the forest. Buck and Spitz limp home, each one badly hurt. The team moves on. One night they fight one last time, and Buck wins, killing Spitz.

IV: Who Is Master?

François and Perrault try to put a dog named Sol-leks in front, but Buck chases him out. They finally let Buck stay. He proves himself a better leader than Spitz was. The team makes record time to Skagway. Then the dogs are passed on to a new mail carrier. Now with a larger pack, Buck fights the fiercest dogs and proves his strength. They carry the mail back to Dawson.

In less than five months, the team has traveled 2,500 miles with very few days of rest. Worn out, they reach Skagway again. Orders say that the worthless dogs must be sold. Buck's team is sold to a family of miners. Charles, his wife Mercedes, and her brother Hal have no experience with sled dogs. They overload the sled. Hal beats the dogs to make them go, even though the load is too heavy. In the end, the dogs must eat horsehide to survive. The dogs are so tired and sick that they cannot move. Buck is near death. John Thornton steps in and makes them leave Buck behind. A quarter of a mile down the trail, the ice breaks and swallows the sled, dogs, and people. John Thornton comforts Buck, who licks his hand.

John Thornton treats Buck so kindly that Buck comes to deeply love his new master. He will do anything for this man who spared his life. He saves Thornton during a fight by attacking the other man. Later he swims out to save Thornton from drowning. Then some men bet that Buck cannot pull a thousand-pound sled alone. He does the job just to please his master.

Thornton uses his earnings from winning the
bet for a new journey. He and his friends
and dogs set out to find a lost gold mine. Buck
begins to feel drawn to the forest. He listens
to the wolves howl. He sometimes runs off into
the woods. On one trip, he makes friends with
a wolf. They run together until Buck remembers
John Thornton. One time, when he returns to
camp, he finds some Yeehats Indians dancing
around the camp. They have killed all the dogs
and men. Buck is so angry that he jumps on
and kills some of the Yeehats. The rest of them
leave. He grieves over John Thornton's death.
Finally, he joins the wolf pack and goes to live
in the wild.

Vocabulary words appear in boldface type and are
footnoted. Specialized or technical words and phrases
appear in lightface type and are footnoted.

Background

Jack London

Jack London is the pen name of John Chaney, born January 12, 1876, in San Francisco. London had a hard childhood, both because of his broken family and the lack of jobs throughout the country. America was in a depression then, and people had little work. London's father also deserted their family when Jack was still a boy.

London, in turn, left school at the age of fourteen to seek adventure. He rode across the country on trains with hobos and spent time reading in public libraries. The little education he got came in libraries in odd moments.

He quit after his first year of college to seek his fortune in the Klondike Gold Rush in 1897. He returned a year later, not having found gold but set on becoming a writer. From then on, London wrote each day. The more than fifty novels he wrote in the last seventeen years of his life show the energy he poured into writing. At one time, he was the highest-paid writer in the country and had great fame, but he never seemed to have enough money.

London's best-known works are his adventure stories, *The Call of the Wild* (1903) and *White Fang* (1906). His respect for and love of the wild forces of nature come through in these popular novels. He seemed fascinated by the idea of force. The law of "tooth and claw," of survival of the fittest, is played out in many of London's books, especially in *The Call of the Wild.*

American readers loved these adventure stories, which made London rich and famous. With the money, he bought a huge ranch in California. Yet his love of adventure and travel never let up. In 1907–08, he sailed around the world on a boat he built himself.

London's heavy drinking and other health problems gradually overtook him. He died on November 22, 1916.

Jack London

1876—Jack London, born as John Chaney, on January 12, in San Francisco.

1895–96—He drops out of high school, but enrolls briefly at the University of California at Berkeley.

1897–98—London joins the Klondike Gold Rush, but returns to California without a fortune, only a desire to write.

1900—London marries Bessie Maddern.

1903—He publishes *The Call of the Wild*—a major success.

1904—*The Sea Wolf* is published.

1906—*White Fang,* another adventure story about a dog, is also widely popular.

1907–08—London sails around the world with his wife on the boat he built, the *Snark*.

1916—He dies after years of weakening health.

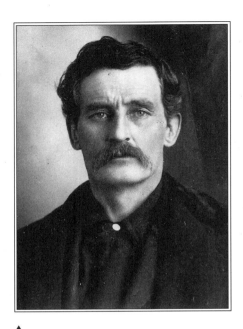

▲
Photograph of Robert Henderson.

The Gold Rush in the Yukon

Gold was first discovered in California in 1848. In the next few years miners worked their way up the coast of Alaska. Finally, in the 1870s and 1880s, miners turned to the Yukon Territory in Canada.

The Yukon Gold Rush began one day in the summer of 1896, when a miner named Robert Henderson scooped up a pan of gravel from a river. He was hoping to find gold. Miners "panned" for gold in riverbeds, sifting through the gravel in search of gold. Henderson found a few gold flakes.

George Carmack and two Native American friends heard that Henderson had found gold. They went to him, curious to see if he had found any more. Henderson chased them off, and they left, angry with him. A few days later, a short distance away at Rabbit Creek, Carmack reached down into the creek and found gold. He found not just a few flakes but several gold nuggets about the size of a quarter. They were rich!

▲
Miners panning for gold in their cabin.

▲
A map of the Yukon 1896–98.

Carmack and his friends rushed to the nearby town of Fortymile to stake a claim. (A claim is the right to mine gold in a certain area.) Once people in town heard how much gold Carmack had found, everyone rushed out to stake claims along Rabbit Creek.

The great gold rush in the Yukon had begun. Just a few days later, after the best claims had been taken, Robert Henderson learned about the gold rush he had begun.

Life in the Yukon

Miners who came to the Yukon found the living conditions hard. Temperatures often hit forty degrees below zero for several days in a row. Miners had a long and difficult journey to reach the Klondike Goldfields in the heart of the Yukon.

First, miners needed steamship tickets to the ports of Dyea and Skagway. From there, they had to cross the Coast Mountains and hike more than five hundred miles to reach Dawson. The journey was as dangerous as it was hard. Each person needed to carry at least one hundred pounds of food.

Jack London, one of the early adventurers to travel to the Klondike, wrote to a friend that he had a thousand pounds of gear. Often he had to make three or four trips back and forth along a trail to carry all of the supplies he needed.

In places, the trail to the Klondike became quite steep. The "Golden Stairs" became one famous part of the trail. Fifteen hundred steps were cut into the ice to help climbers make it to the top of Chilkoot Pass. To climb up the stairs with fifty pounds of supplies took miners about six hours—and each miner had to make the trip about twelve times to carry over all of his supplies!

To make his story real, London uses the names of actual places in *The Call of the Wild*, such as Dawson, Chilcoot Pass, Lake Bennett, and Skagway.

A long line of miners packing up Chilkoot Pass.

▲
Weary miners stop for a rest along the trail.

Sled Dogs

Dog sledding was introduced by the Eskimos, who relied on it as the main form of transportation. They bred special Eskimo dogs and Siberian huskies for the job of pulling sleds across the snow. Usually five, seven, or nine dogs pulled a sled. One dog always leads, and the other dogs are hitched side-by-side.

The driver of the sled is called the musher. He or she controls the dogs by talking to them, ordering them to slow down or hurry up, turn or stop. A good dog team can travel at about twenty miles per hour—about the speed of a slow-moving car.

At the time Jack London lived and wrote, dog sledding was still an important form of transportation in the Yukon. In order to survive, miners had to carry great amounts of food and clothing over miles of snowy country in arctic cold. Dogsleds were used to make carrying food and clothing a little easier.

▲

Settlements during the Gold Rush were much like this boat-building camp at Abbot Cove, Lake Bennett.

The Story of George Williams's Amazing Journey

When gold was first discovered in the Yukon, traders knew food shortages would come too. In order to have enough food for all the miners flocking to the Yukon, a man named George Williams made a five-hundred-mile, cross-country journey in the middle of winter with a Native American boy. The scene was very much like the one London wrote about in *The Call of the Wild* and his classic story "To Build a Fire."

Williams and the boy set off in January with a dog team. Everyone thought their chances were almost hopeless, but still necessary. It was only a matter of time before the feet of the dogs became cut and sore because of the ice. Williams and the boy had to melt the ice on the dogs' paws with their breath so they could keep moving.

By March, all of the dogs had died of starvation or freezing. Williams and the boy were left to walk and eventually were caught in a terrible snowstorm. For three days they lived in a snowbank. Williams's legs were so frostbitten he could no longer walk.

Finally, the boy left on his own and reached the outpost of Dyea. After getting help, he went back to get Williams. By the time Williams arrived in town, he died without saying a word. The Native American boy delivered the message that more food would be needed in the Yukon and helped to prevent starvation for thousands of miners flocking to the area.

Miners carrying loads of canned food along the trail. ▼

A CLASSIC RETELLING

The Call *of the*
WILD

CHAPTER 1

Into the Primitive

Buck did not read the newspapers, or he would have known that trouble was coming. Trouble was in store for every strong dog with warm, long hair, from Canada to California. Because men had found a yellow metal,[1] ships and trains were rushing men to the Northland. These men wanted dogs. They wanted heavy dogs with strong muscles and furry coats to keep off the frost.

Buck lived at a big house in the sun-kissed Santa Clara Valley. Judge Miller's place, it was called. It stood among trees and wide lawns. In back there were horse stables, servants' cabins,

---

[1] yellow metal—London refers to gold and the gold rush that took place in the Klondike area of Canada in the 1890s.

orchards, and berry patches. There was a water tank where Judge Miller's boys swam. And Buck ruled over all this land. Here he had lived for all the four years of his life. It was true, there were other dogs, but they didn't count. They lived in the **kennels**[2] or in the house. But Buck was neither house-dog nor kennel-dog. The whole **realm**[3] was his.

He jumped into the swimming tank or went hunting with the Judge's sons. He took long walks with the Judge's daughters. At night he lay at the Judge's feet before the roaring fire. He guarded the Judge's grandsons on their trips to the berry patches. He was king over all the creeping, crawling, flying things of Judge Miller's place, humans included.

B uck's father, Elmo, a huge St. Bernard,[4] had been the Judge's best friend. Buck had now taken his father's place. He was not as large as his father— he weighed only one hundred and forty pounds, for his mother had been a Scotch shepherd[5] dog.

---

[2] **kennels**—shelters for dogs.

[3] **realm**—kingdom; domain.

[4] St. Bernard—a very large breed of dog.

[5] Scotch shepherd—a breed of guide dogs from Scotland.

Buck had grown up with pride, like a country gentleman, but he was not lazy. He hunted outdoors and loved to swim. This was the kind of dog Buck was in the fall of 1897, when the Klondike gold strike dragged men from all over the world into the frozen North.

He trusted men he knew, but when the stranger took the rope, he began to growl.

Manuel was one of the gardener's helpers at Judge Miller's place. Buck did not know that Manuel was not to be trusted. He had lost money gambling, and he needed some cash to feed his family. One night when the Judge was not home, Manuel took Buck on a long walk. He walked Buck all the way to a park and stopped to talk to a man. The man handed Manuel money and asked him to put a rope around Buck's neck. Manuel wrapped a rope around Buck's neck and said, "Twist it if you need to choke him."

Buck stood quietly. He trusted people he knew, but when the stranger took the rope, he began to growl. To his surprise, the rope tightened around his neck. He sprang at the man, who grabbed him by the throat and threw him on his back. The rope tightened again. Buck struggled, more angry than he had ever been—he had never been treated this way. The man threw him onto the baggage car of a train, and away they went.

Buck's tongue hurt, and he felt like a kidnapped king. The man saw his angry eyes and tried to grab his throat again. Buck bit the man's hand, so he was choked again, until his senses left him. The next day, they got off in San Francisco. The man took Buck, who was still dazed and in pain, to a little shed behind a **saloon**[6] on the waterfront. The man grumbled that he only got fifty dollars for delivering the dog and hurt his hand doing it. The saloonkeeper helped him take the collar off Buck's neck and put him in a cage-like crate.

There Buck lay for the rest of the night. He could not understand what it all meant. What did they want with him, these strange men? Why were they keeping him in this crate? Several times during the night he heard a noise and jumped up, hoping to see the Judge. Each time it was only the saloonkeeper. When Buck saw him, his joyful bark would become a growl. But the saloonkeeper left him alone.

---

[6] **saloon**—a place where alcoholic drinks are served.

In the morning, four men came and picked up the crate. Buck barked at them through the bars. They laughed and poked sticks at him. After that, the crate passed through many hands. Buck rode in a wagon, then a truck, then a boat, then a train, and finally a wagon again. For two days and nights this wagon dragged along, and for two days and nights Buck did not eat or drink. His throat and tongue hurt from lack of water. His eyes turned red. He became such an angry beast during this terrible experience that the Judge himself would not have known him. The deliverymen felt glad to be rid of him when they reached Seattle. They carried the crate into a small back yard. A man in a red sweater came out and signed the driver's book. Buck snarled at the man and pushed against the bars. The man smiled and got an ax and a club.

"You going to take him out now?" the driver asked.

"Sure," the man said. The other four ran to a safe place as he pried the crate open with the ax. Buck banged against the crate and bit the wood.

"Now, you red-eyed devil," the man said when he had made a hole big enough for Buck to fit through. Buck's mouth foamed. He jumped at the man in the red sweater. Just as he was about to bite the man, he felt a shock. He fell to the ground. He had never been struck by a club in his life. He got up and leaped at the man. The shock came again and he fell to the ground. A dozen times he charged. Each time the club smashed him down.

After the next blow he crawled to his feet. Blood flowed from his nose, mouth, and ears and matted his beautiful fur. The man charged him and hit him harder on the nose. The pain grew worse than ever. Buck roared and ran at the man, but the club caught him under the jaw and flipped him over. For the last time he rushed. The man struck so hard that Buck could do nothing but lie there. He could not even think.

"He's no **slouch**[7] at **dog-breaking**.[8] That's what I say," one of the men on the wall cried out. Buck's senses came back to him but not his strength. He lay where he had fallen and watched the man in the red sweater.

"Answers to the name of Buck," the man said, reading the saloonkeeper's letter. "Well, Buck, my boy, we've had our little contest. You've learned

---

[7] **slouch**—a lazy person.

[8] **dog-breaking**—making a dog more obedient using discipline or force.

your place. Be a good dog and all will go well. Be a bad dog, and I'll **whale**[9] the stuffin' out of you. Understand?"

As he spoke, he patted the head he had pounded. Buck's hair stood on end, but he did not make a sound. Then the man brought Buck water, and Buck lapped it up. Later Buck ate a meal of raw meat from the man's hand. He was beaten, and he knew it, but he was not broken. He saw that he stood no chance against a man with a club. He had learned the lesson, and in all his life he never forgot it. He began to understand **primitive**[10] law.

He was beaten, and he knew it, but he was not broken. He saw that he stood no chance against a man with a club.

As the days went by, other dogs came. Some came in crates and others at the ends of ropes. Some came easily. Some came roaring as he had come. The man in the red sweater broke them all. Now and then other men came and talked to the man in the red sweater. Money passed between them, and they took one or more of the dogs away with them. Buck did not know where they went,

---

[9] **whale**—beat or hit.

[10] **primitive**—crude; from an early age of the world's being.

for they never came back. He began to fear his own future.

Soon his time came. A man with a wrinkled face arrived. He spoke in a strange way that Buck did not always understand. When he saw Buck he said, "What a **bully**[11] dog! How much?"

"Three hundred, and a good deal at that, Perrault," said the man in the red sweater. Perrault knew dogs. When he looked at Buck he knew this dog was one in a thousand. Perrault delivered **dispatches**[12] for the Canadian government. Buck could help him bring the messages more quickly.

Buck saw money pass between Perrault and the man in the red sweater. Soon Perrault led him away, along with Curly, an easy-going **Newfoundland.**[13] That was the last he saw of the man in the red sweater. He and Curly ended up on a ship called the *Narwhal*. As they looked back at the city of Seattle, they did not know they would never see the Southland again.

---

[11] **bully**—a slang word for "good."

[12] **dispatches**—reports sent with speed.

[13] **Newfoundland**—a large breed of dog with a thick coat, usually from the Newfoundland province of Canada.

Perrault turned the dogs over to a dark-skinned giant called François. He took Buck and Curly down to a lower deck of the boat to join two other dogs. One of them tried to steal Buck's food, but François's whip stopped him. The other dog, Dave, kept to himself. When the boat rolled and bucked, they all **yelped**[14] in fear, but Dave just yawned and went to sleep again.

Buck grew to respect Perrault and François. They were both fair, calm men, but they knew dogs too well to be fooled by them. They **tended**[15] to the dogs during the long voyage. Each day was just like the next, only colder. Finally the ship stopped moving and grew still. The dogs knew a change was coming. François leashed them and brought them on deck. At the first step onto the cold deck, Buck's feet sank into a white mushy something very much like mud. He sprang back with a snort. More of this white stuff was falling through the air. He shook himself, but more of it fell upon him. He sniffed it, then licked some of it on his tongue. It bit like fire then was gone. This puzzled him. Everyone watching Buck began to laugh. He felt ashamed. He did not know why, for it was his first snow.

---

[14] **yelped**—a dog's cry; barked.
[15] **tended**—took care of.

The Law of Club and Fang

Buck's first day on the beach was like a nightmare. Every hour was filled with shock. He had been jerked from the heart of city life and flung into the heart of things **primordial.**[1] No lazy, sun-kissed life was this. Here was no peace, no rest, and no safety. Buck had to stay alert because these dogs were not town dogs and men. They knew no law but the law of club and fang.[2]

He had never seen dogs fight as these dogs fought. They acted like wolves. His first lesson

---

[1] **primordial**—from the beginning of the world.

[2] club and fang—London refers to the man's club and the dog's tooth as symbols of the fight for survival in the wild.

taught him things he could not forget. Curly was the victim. One night they were camped near a log store. She, in her friendly way, moved toward a smaller husky dog. The dog leaped at her like a flash. He ripped Curly's face open from eye to jaw. After the first leap, thirty or forty huskies ran to the spot. They licked their chops and stood around the fighters in a silent circle. Curly rushed in, but the husky struck her again. He pushed her with his chest and knocked her off her feet. This is what the other dogs had waited for. They quickly closed in on her, snarling and yelping. She screamed in pain under the mass of bodies.

Curly lay there limp and lifeless in the bloody snow. The dogs had almost torn her to pieces.

Buck watched in shock. A snow-white dog named Spitz was laughing. Then François swung an ax handle into the mess of dogs. Three men with clubs helped to scatter them, but it was too late. Curly lay there limp and lifeless in the bloody snow. The dogs had almost torn her to pieces.

This scene would come back to Buck many times in his sleep. Now he knew the way it was. No fair play. Once down, that was the end of you. Well, he would never let them push him down. He saw Spitz laugh again, and from that moment Buck hated him.

Before he could forget Curly's dying, Buck got another shock. François tied him up with straps and buckles. It was a harness like the ones he had seen on horses back home. Just as the horses worked there, he was to work here, pulling François on a sled to get firewood. It hurt his pride to be treated as a workhorse, but he went along and did his best. He felt the whip when he did the wrong thing, or else he felt Dave **nipping**[3] him from behind. Spitz was the leader, and he jerked one way or the other to show Buck which way to go. Buck quickly learned to stop at "ho" and to go at "mush." He learned to swing wide on the bends and stay clear of the sled when it shot downhill.

"Three very good dogs," François told Perrault. "That Buck, I teach him quick as anything."

By afternoon, Perrault had bought two more dogs, Billee and Joe. Billee was always happy, and Joe was always angry. Buck welcomed them both, but Dave ignored them, and Spitz attacked them. Billee cried when Spitz bit into his side, but Joe fought back.

---

[3] **nipping**—biting.

By evening, Perrault returned with another dog, an old husky with a torn face and only one eye. He was called Sol-leks, which means The Angry One. Like Dave, he asked nothing and gave nothing. Buck would soon learn that these two dogs lived for one thing only: pulling a dog sled.

That night Buck again faced the problem of where to find the warmest place to sleep. The tent looked warm, so he tried to go inside, but Perrault and François threw pans and spoons at him to chase him out. A chill wind blew. He lay down and tried to sleep, but the cold drove him to his feet. He walked around looking for a warm place. He searched for his teammates but could not find any of them in the camp. Then he began to circle the tent. He felt the snow give way under his legs, and he sank down. Something moved under his feet. He jumped back, but a friendly yelp made him less afraid. He looked down and saw a hole in the snow. Billee lay there, curled in a ball. He looked warm and happy and tried to lick Buck's face.

Buck had learned another lesson. He now knew how the huskies kept warm at night. Buck chose a spot. With much fuss, he dug a hole for himself.

The heat from his body filled the space, and he soon fell asleep. The day had been long, so he slept deeply, though he had bad dreams. He did not open his eyes until he heard the noises of the waking camp. At first he did not know where he was. It had snowed during the night, and the snow buried him. He feared he was in a trap, even though he had never seen one before. This fear of traps had come to many dogs in the past, and now it came to him. His body shook. With a loud snarl he jumped up into the daylight. The snow flew about him in a cloud. He saw the camp and knew where he was when he heard François shout to Perrault, "What did I say? That Buck sure learn quick as anything." Perrault nodded. As **courier**[4] for the Canadian government, he had important messages to deliver. He needed the best dogs and felt proud he had chosen Buck.

Three more huskies—Dub, Pike, and Dolly— joined the team within an hour. All nine dogs were soon harnessed and swinging up the trail. Buck felt glad to go. The work was hard, but he liked it. He was surprised at the eagerness of the team, especially Dave and Sol-leks. The harness had changed

---

[4] **courier**—a messenger carrying important papers.

them. They were suddenly alert and cared deeply about the work. The **toil**[5] of the **traces**[6] was all they lived for and the only thing in which they took joy. Dave was the wheeler or sled dog. Buck pulled in front of him. Sol-leks was next. The rest stood between him and the leader, Spitz. Buck worked between Dave and Sol-leks so they could teach him, and they did a good job of it.

It was a hard day's run up the canyon. They had to cross **glaciers**[7] and snowdrifts hundreds of feet deep. They had to cross the great Chilcoot Divide, which stands between the salt water and the sad, lonely North. They made good time down a chain of lakes and late that night pulled into the huge camp at Lake Bennett. Thousands of gold-seekers were building boats to use when the snow thawed. Buck made his hole in the snow and slept soundly. Morning came too early and he soon stood beside his mates at the sled.

That day they made forty miles. The next day they had to make their own trail, so they worked harder but made poorer time. This went on for days. Perrault went ahead of the team, packing

---

[5] **toil**—work.

[6] **traces**—straps that attach an animal to a sled.

[7] **glaciers**—rivers of ice moving very slowly.

the snow with his shoes to make it easier for them. François guided the sled. Sometimes they changed places.

Day after day Buck toiled in the traces. The crew always left before sunrise and set up camp after sunset. They ate their bit of fish and crawled to sleep in the snow. Buck never got enough food. The smaller dogs, who were used to life in the wild, did well on one pound of fish, but Buck was still hungry. What's worse, if Buck ate too slowly and they finished first, they robbed him of the rest of his dinner. He began to eat as fast as they did and then take their leftovers. He never got caught.

Learning to steal changed Buck. It made him fit to survive in the Northland.

Learning to steal changed Buck. It made him fit to survive in the Northland. At the same time, it marked the **decay**[8] of his moral nature.[9] What worked in the Southland, under the law of love, did not work in the Northland, under the law of club and fang. Not that Buck thought about it. He simply changed to live a new way of life. He did

---

[8] **decay**—rotting or death.
[9] moral nature—sense of right and wrong.

not steal for fun but out of hunger, and he did not rob openly but secretly, for fear of club and fang. The changes took place quickly. His muscles became hard as iron. He learned to live with pain. He could eat anything. His sight and scent became **keen.**[10] He learned to break the ice to drink from the water hole. He found he could tell which way the wind would blow at night and choose a sheltered place to dig his nest.

> *Buck learned not only by what happened but by his own instincts. He seemed to remember when his breed was wild and ranged in packs.*

Buck learned not only by what happened but by his own **instincts.**[11] He seemed to remember when his **breed**[12] was wild and ranged in packs. He learned to fight as if he had to for his meat. He knew the survival skills of his ancestors. And on still, cold nights, he pointed his nose at a star and howled. It sounded like his wolflike ancestors howling down through the centuries and through him. His song was their song. The ancient song came through him

---

[10] **keen**—sharp or clear.

[11] **instincts**—skills known but not learned; things a person or animal does by nature, without thinking.

[12] **breed**—a group of animals that look alike and share a set of grandparents.

and he came into his own again. And he came because men had found a yellow metal in the North, and because Manuel's **wages**[13] could not feed his family.

---

[13] **wages**—money paid for work done.

CHAPTER III

The Dominant Beast

The wish for **dominance**[1] was strong in Buck. In this fierce new life, it grew and grew. His new **cunning**[2] gave him a sense of control. He did not pick fights, even with Spitz. On the other hand, Spitz, who saw him as a dangerous enemy, bullied him whenever he could. He kept trying to start a fight that could only end in the death of one or the other.

One snowy night, Perrault and François lit their fire and set up camp on the ice of a lake. Buck made his nest under a rock. He hated to leave the warm

---

[1] **dominance**—being the best of a group, in command.
[2] **cunning**—slyness, craftiness, skill at lying.

nest to eat his dinner. When he did, he came back to find Spitz inside the nest. Now the beast in him roared. Buck sprang upon Spitz in a fury. François rushed out to see what happened. He cheered Buck on and said, "Get that thief!" Spitz looked eager to fight as Buck circled around him. Just then, a pack of more than a hundred starving huskies crept into camp to watch the fight. Perrault and François swung clubs at them, but the wild dogs fought back. They were crazed by the smell of food. Perrault found one with his head in the **grub**[3] box. He hit the dog and the box spilled onto the ground. Twenty hungry **brutes**[4] rushed to get the bread and bacon. Clubs fell upon them. They howled but kept eating until the last crumb was gone.

As soon as the team dogs came out of their nests, the wild dogs attacked them. Never had Buck seen such dogs. Their hides barely hung on their bones. Their eyes blazed. Drool dripped from

[3] **grub**—food.
[4] **brutes**—beasts.

their fangs. The hunger-madness made them terrifying. There was no stopping them. The wild dogs drove the team dogs against the cliff. Three huskies attacked Buck and cut his head and shoulders. Billee cried. Dave and Sol-leks fought bravely side by side. Joe broke one dog's leg and then Pike leaped upon the injured dog and broke its neck. Buck turned and sank his teeth into the throat of another dog. The warm taste of blood made him fearless. He flung himself upon another. At the same time he felt teeth sink into his own throat. It was Spitz, attacking from the side.

Perrault and François had cleaned out their part of the camp. They hurried over to save their sled dogs, swinging their clubs. The wave of beasts rolled back, and Buck shook himself free. Then the men went back to chase more huskies away from the grub, leaving the team dogs alone again. Billee, scared into bravery, sprang through the circle and ran away over the ice. Pike and Dub followed, with the rest behind. Buck braced himself, for he saw Spitz rushing upon him. Once off his feet, he knew there was no hope for him. But after the shock of Spitz's charge, he joined the flight out on the lake.

Later, the nine team-dogs gathered together in the forest. Every one of them was hurt in four or five places. Some were hurt badly. Dub had a broken hind leg. Dolly had a torn throat. Joe had lost an eye. The good-natured Billee, with an ear chewed to pieces, cried through the night. At daybreak, they limped back to camp. They found the two men angry and **brooding.**[5] Half their food supply was gone. The huskies had chewed through the sled lashings. Nothing **edible**[6] had escaped them. They had eaten Perrault's moose-hide **moccasins,**[7] chunks out of the leather traces, and even the end of François's whip. He turned away from the whip to look over his wounded dogs.

"Ah, my friends," he said softly, "Maybe it make you mad dogs, those many bites. Maybe all mad dog. What you think, eh, Perrault?"

The courier shook his head. With four hundred miles of trail between him and Dawson, he could not afford to have mad dogs. Within two hours, the men made some repairs and got the team on its way. The dogs struggled painfully over the hardest part of the trail they had yet covered.

---

[5] **brooding**—in a serious, thoughtful mood.
[6] **edible**—able to be eaten.
[7] **moccasins**—soft leather shoes.

The Thirty Mile River was wide open. Its wild water would not freeze, except in the quiet places. It took six days to cover those thirty miles. Every step brought risk of life to dog and man. A dozen times, Perrault broke through the ice bridges. He pulled himself out by his pole each time. But a cold snap was on, and it fell to fifty degrees below zero. So each time he broke through he had to build a fire and dry his clothes to save his own life.

Every step brought risk of life to dog and man. A dozen times, Perrault broke through the ice bridges.

Nothing stopped him. That's why he had been chosen as a government courier. He took risks, struggling on from dawn until dark. He sometimes took the sled along rim ice that bent under foot. Once, the sled broke through, with Dave and Buck. They were half-frozen and almost drowned by the time they were dragged out. It took a warming fire to save them. They had to run around the fire, sweating and thawing, close to the flames.

At another time Spitz fell through. Most of the team was dragged in, all the way up to Buck. He dug his paws into the slippery ice and pulled back with all his strength. The only escape was up a cliff. Perrault climbed it and then hoisted the dogs up by rope. François came last with the sled and load. Then they had to use the ropes to lower the dogs safely onto the other side. It took all day to go a quarter of a mile. By the time they got to the next town, the dogs were all tired. But Perrault wanted to make up for lost time. They covered thirty-five to forty miles a day for the next few days.

Buck's feet were not as hard as the feet of the huskies. All day he limped in pain. At night, he could not move, and François had to bring him his fish. He also rubbed Buck's feet each night after supper. He even cut off the tops of his moccasins to make four moc-

At night, he could not move, and François had to bring him his fish. He also rubbed Buck's feet each night after supper.

casins for Buck. This was a great relief. One morning, when François forgot to put them on him, Buck lay on his back, waving his feet in the air. Even Perrault had to grin. Once Buck's feet finally grew used to the trail, they threw the foot-gear away.

One day as they were getting ready to leave, Dolly suddenly went mad. She let out a long wolf howl, then sprang for Buck. He had never seen a dog go mad, yet he knew enough to run away from her. He raced with the panting Dolly, who was one leap behind him. He ran fast out of fear.

She ran fast out of madness. He went through the woods and crossed the river to first one island, then another. François called to him and he looped back, hoping the man would save him. François held the ax in his hand. As Buck shot past him, the ax crashed down upon mad Dolly's head.

Now Spitz saw his chance. He sprang upon Buck, tearing the flesh to the bone.

Buck slumped against the sled, sobbing for breath. Now Spitz saw his chance. He sprang upon Buck, tearing the flesh to the bone. But he did not get any farther. François's lash fell upon Spitz, who got the worst whipping of any dog yet.

"He's one devil, that Spitz," said Perrault. "Some day him kill that Buck."

"That Buck two devils," François replied. "Some fine day him get mad and chew that Spitz all up and spit him out on the snow. Sure. I know."

From then on it was war between them. Buck was not soft like other Southland dogs Spitz had known. The club of the man in the red sweater had made Buck cunning. He was willing to wait for just the right moment to take Spitz's place as leader. He wanted it because it was his nature. He had been gripped by the pride of the trail and trace. It was the pride that makes dogs willing to die joyfully in the harness and breaks their hearts if they are cut out of the harness. This was the pride of Dave as wheel-dog and of Sol-leks as he pulled with all his strength. It was the pride that made Spitz **thrash**[8] the dogs who were lazy or slow. It was this pride that made him fear Buck as a lead dog. And this was Buck's pride too.

Buck tried to protect the other dogs and become their leader. When Pike hid one morning, Spitz searched all over, snarling with anger until he found him. Buck flew in between them so Spitz could not punish Pike. François had to beat Buck to turn him away from the fight. In the days that followed, Buck continued to come between Spitz and the other dogs, but only when François was not around. Soon the dogs did not want to do as they were told. The team went from bad to worse. There was trouble coming, and at the bottom of it was Buck.

Finally they reached Dawson one afternoon. Here were many men and dogs, all at work. The dogs **hauled**[9] cabin logs and firewood. They took

---

[8] **thrash**—strike over and over.

[9] **hauled**—carried, moved.

loads to the mines. They did the work that horses did in the Santa Clara Valley. Here and there Buck met Southland dogs, but they were mostly the wild wolf-husky breed. Every night they howled an **eerie**[10] chant, and Buck loved to join in the song.

The aurora borealis[11] flamed coldly overhead. The stars leaped in a frost dance. The land froze under its cloak of snow. This song of the huskies might have been life breaking through the cold. But they sang it in a pleading, sad key, with long wails and sobs. So it seemed more like a song of the struggle for survival. It was an old song, as old as the breed itself. Buck felt stirred when he moaned and sobbed it. He sang of the pain of living that was the pain of his wild fathers. His fears were their fears. The song stirred some part of him that remembered the age of fire and roof.[12] He knew the raw beginnings of life in the howling ages.

A week after they pulled into Dawson, they dropped down to the Yukon Trail and turned toward the ocean. Perrault was carrying dispatches even more important than those he had brought in. Also,

---

[10] **eerie**—causing a feeling of mystery and fear.

[11] aurora borealis—the northern lights, an unexplained streak of light that appears regularly in the night sky near the North Pole.

[12] age of fire and roof—the period of history when humans first discovered fire and found shelter.

the travel pride had gripped him. He wanted to make the record trip of the year. It looked as though he could. The dogs had rested for a week. The trail was hard packed. And the police had placed supplies of grub along the way, so they could travel light.

They made good time, but not without trouble. The revolt led by Buck had destroyed the unity of the team. The dogs no longer worked together as a team. And no longer did the dogs fear Spitz. Pike robbed him of half a fish one night and gulped it down with Buck as his guard. Another night Dub and Joe fought Spitz. Even Billee was less good-natured with Spitz. As for Buck, he never came near Spitz without growling. In fact, he acted like a bully.

The dogs also argued amongst themselves more. François lashed them, but it did no good. While he backed up Spitz, Buck backed up the rest of the team. He knew Buck was behind the problems, yet Buck worked hard in the traces and never got caught making trouble. He loved his work pulling the sled almost as much as he loved starting fights among his mates.

One night after supper, Dub found a rabbit. He tried to catch it but missed. In a second, the whole team was in full chase. Fifty police dogs from a nearby camp heard and joined them. The rabbit sped down the river, turned off into a small creek, and went up the frozen bed. It ran over the snow while the dogs chased behind. Buck led the pack of sixty around bend after bend.

There is a joy that marks the peak of life. It comes to the artist as he paints. It comes to the soldier, war-mad on a field. It came to Buck leading the pack, sounding the old wolf-cry, chasing down the food that was alive and that fled before him in the moonlight. He was calling out to his animal instincts, those that went back to the dawn of Time. He felt the **surging**[13] of life, the perfect joy of each muscle and joint, of everything that was not death. It was all aglow and moving. It was flying under the stars and over the face of dead matter that did not move.

Meanwhile, Spitz left the pack and took a short-cut. Buck did not know this, and as he rounded the bend, the rabbit still flitting before him, he saw another larger animal leap from a high bank into the path of the rabbit. It was Spitz. The rabbit could

---

[13] **surging**—swelling, rising.

not turn. As the white teeth broke its back in mid-air, it screamed as loudly as a man would scream. At the sound of this, the cry of Life plunging down into the grip of Death, the full pack raised its cry.

Buck did not cry out. He drove in upon Spitz, shoulder to shoulder, so hard that he missed the throat. They rolled over and over in the snow. Spitz got back on his feet, slashing Buck down the shoulder and leaping clear. Twice his teeth clipped together, like the steel jaws of a trap.

In a flash Buck knew it. The time had come. It was to the death.

In a flash Buck knew it. The time had come. It was to the death. Calm came over the whiteness. Nothing moved. Not a leaf shook. The breaths of the dogs rose slowly in the frosty air. They had made short work of the rabbit, these wolflike dogs. They, too, were silent as they drew into a circle.

Spitz was a practiced fighter. He never rushed until he was ready to receive a rush. When Buck tried to sink his teeth into the neck of the big white dog, fang clashed against fang, and lips were cut and bleeding. Time and time again he tried for the snow-white throat. Each time Spitz slashed him and got away.

Spitz was untouched, while Buck was bloody and panting hard. All the while, the silent, wolfish circle waited to finish off whichever dog went down. As Buck grew winded, Spitz took to rushing. Once Buck went over but caught himself in midair. But Buck had a quality that made for greatness—imagination. He rushed for the shoulder, but in the end swept low and in. His teeth closed on Spitz's left **foreleg.**[14] There was a crunch of breaking bone, and the white dog faced him on three legs. Three times he tried to knock him over. Then he repeated the trick and broke the right foreleg. Despite the pain, Spitz struggled to keep up. He saw the silent circle closing in upon him. He had seen the same thing many times before, only this time he was the one who was beaten.

There was no hope for him. The circle came in until he could feel their breath on him. Buck could see their eyes fixed upon him. A pause seemed to fall. Every animal stood still as though turned to stone. Spitz staggered back and forth, growling as if to scare off his own death. Then Buck sprang in

---

[14] **foreleg**—front leg.

and out, knocking him down. The dark circle became a dot on the moon-flooded snow as Spitz disappeared from view. Buck stood and looked on, the beast who had finally made his kill.

CHAPTER IV

Who Is Master?

"Eh? What I say? I spoke true when I say that Buck two devils."

This was François's speech next morning when he saw that Spitz was missing and Buck was covered with wounds. He brought him to the fire and doctored the wounds. "Now we make good time. No more Spitz, no more trouble."

While Perrault packed up and loaded the sled, the dog driver harnessed the dogs. Buck **trotted**[1] up to the place Spitz would have stood as leader. François, not seeing him, brought Sol-leks to that spot. He thought Sol-leks the best lead dog left.

---

[1] **trotted**—jogged.

Buck disagreed. He sprang upon Sol-leks in a **fury**[2] and stood in his place.

"Eh?" François cried, slapping his thighs. "Look at that Buck. Him kill that Spitz, him think to take the job." He told Buck to go away, but Buck would not budge. He dragged him to one side and put Sol-leks in his place again. The old dog did not like it, and showed that he was afraid of Buck. François did not give in, but when he turned his back, the two dogs traded places.

> *François threw down the club, but Buck still would not take his place. He wanted to be the leader.*

François was angry. He came back with a club in his hand. Buck remembered the man in the red sweater. He stepped back slowly, snarling just out of range of the club.

The driver went about his work, and he called to Buck when he was ready to put him in his old place. Buck retreated from him again and again. François threw down the club, but Buck still would not take his place. He wanted to be the leader. It was his right, and he would not take any less.

Perrault and François chased him around for the better part of an hour. Finally they saw that

---

[2] **fury**—rage.

time was flying. François scratched his head. He finally looked at Perrault and grinned. They knew they were beaten. François went up to where Sol-leks stood and called to Buck. Buck laughed, as dogs laugh, yet stood back. François put Sol-leks in his old place. The teams stood ready to go. François called to Buck again. Once more, Buck laughed but kept away.

"Throw down the club," Perrault shouted. François did. Finally Buck trotted in, laughing, and swung into his place at the head of the team. His traces were fastened, the sled broken out, and with both men running they dashed out onto the river trail.

In a flash, Buck took up the job of leadership. He showed the ability for quick thinking and quick acting. He was even better than Spitz, for whom François had seen no equal. But it was in giving the law and making his mates live up to it that Buck did best. He made Pike pull more of the weight. He punished Joe for being in a bad mood. At last the whole team perked up again and worked together as one. Soon two more dogs, Teek and Koona, were added. Buck swiftly took them in.

"Never such a dog as that Buck!" François cried. "Him worth one thousand dollar, eh, Perrault?"

Perrault nodded. He was ahead of the record, and gaining day by day. The trail was in good shape. There was no new snow. It was not too cold. So the men took turns running and riding and made few stops. The Thirty Mile River was coated with ice, so they covered in one day what had taken them ten days to cover coming in. On the last night of the second week, they dropped down the sea slope with the lights of Skagway at their feet. It was a record run. Each day for fourteen days, they had averaged forty miles.

The dogs rested as François and Perrault bragged about town. Next came official orders. François called Buck to him. The man threw his arms around him and wept over him. And that was the last of François and Perrault. Like other men, they passed out of Buck's life for good.

After that, a Scotch[3] man took charge of Buck and his mates. They and a dozen other dog teams started back over the trail to Dawson. It was hard work each day, with a heavy load behind, for this was the mail train. It carried word from the world

---

[3] Scotch—from Scotland, a country in the north of Great Britain.

to the men who mined gold under the shadow of the North Pole.

Buck did not enjoy the work, but he took pride in it. One day was very much like another. Each morning the cooks built fires and everyone ate breakfast. Then, while some broke camp, others hitched the dogs. They were on the trail an hour or so before dawn. At night, camp was made. Some cut firewood or made beds, some carried water or ice for the cooks, and some fed the dogs. After they ate the fish, they loafed around for an hour or so. There were fierce fighters among them, but Buck had won the battles with the toughest. This made Buck the master of the dogs. When he showed his teeth, they got out of the way.

There were fierce fighters among them, but Buck had won the battles with the toughest. This made Buck the master of the dogs.

At night, he often lay near the fire and dreamed. Sometimes he thought of Judge Miller's house in the sun-kissed valley. But more often he thought of the man in the red sweater, the death of Curly, and the great fight with Spitz. He thought of the good things he had eaten or would like to eat.

He was not homesick. The Sunland was very dim and had no power over him. Far more powerfully, he remembered his fathers who came before him. They had given him memories of things he had never seen. Their habits and instincts came alive in him.

Sometimes as he crouched there, blinking at the flames, it seemed that the flames were of another fire. He saw an earlier time and a different kind of man. This man[4] had short legs and long arms and long hair all over his body. His head slanted back. He was all but naked and did not stand erect. He leaned forward from the hips, on legs that bent at the knees. He seemed almost catlike and alert and fearful. Sometimes this man squatted by the fire and slept. Beyond this fire, Buck could see many coals, two by two, which he knew to be the eyes of great beasts. He could hear them crashing through the grass. Dreaming there by the riverbank, these sounds and sights of another world would make the hair rise along his back. He would growl until

[4] this man—London refers to prehistoric man, basing his description on Darwin's theory of evolution.

the cook shouted at him. Then he would get up and yawn, pretending he had been asleep.

It was a hard trip with the heavy mail behind them. They should have had a long rest when they reached Dawson. But in two days they left again. The dogs were tired and it snowed every day. Since the start of winter they had traveled eighteen hundred miles, pulling sleds all the way. Buck was tired, but he kept the crew going. Billee cried at night, Joe was more grumpy than ever, and Sol-leks did not want to talk to anyone. But it was Dave who suffered most of all. He could not get up once he sat down at night. Sometimes when jerked in the traces, he cried out in pain. The drivers could find nothing wrong with him. They talked it over one night. Someone brought him to the fire to see if he had any broken bones. They could find nothing, but something was wrong inside.

By the time they got to the next town, Dave was falling down a lot. So they let him run free behind the sled for awhile. Sick as he was, Dave did not like being taken out. He did not like giving Sol-leks the job he had held for so long. Pride was his. Sick and nearly dying, he still could not let another dog do his work.

When the sled started, Dave stumbled in the soft snow along the beaten trail. All the while, he attacked Sol-leks with his teeth, rushing against him and trying to push him away. He tried to leap between Sol-leks and the sled. All the while, he yelped with pain. The driver tried to whip him, but had not the heart to strike very hard. Dave refused to run quietly on the trail behind the sled. He ran through the drifts alongside the trail, where the going was the hardest. He ran until he could not run any more. Finally he fell in the slow, howling as the long train of sleds went by.

With the last of his strength, he staggered along behind until the train stopped. Then he found his own sled and stood beside Sol-leks. When they tried to move on, the sled would not go. Dave had bitten Sol-leks's traces. He was standing in front of the sled in his proper place.

The driver talked with his friends. They said that a dog's heart can break if you take away its work, even the work that will kill it. They wanted Dave to die happy in the traces, since they knew he would die anyway. So they harnessed him again.

He fell down and was dragged many times, and once the sled fell upon him, so he limped after that.

Still, Dave made it to the next camp. The driver made a place for him to sleep by the fire. Morning found him too weak to travel. He tried to crawl to the sled, but he kept falling. He would try to stand up and take a step, then fall again. He crawled his way to where his mates stood. He had to move his front feet and drag his body forward. Finally, his strength left him. The last his mates saw of him, he lay there in the snow, howling as they passed out of sight behind a stretch of trees. Here the train stopped. The Scotch driver walked back to the camp. A shot rang out. The man came back quickly. Then the whips snapped, the bells rang, and the sleds went on. But Buck knew, and every dog knew, what had taken place behind the belt of river trees.

CHAPTER V

The Toil of Trace and Trail

Thirty days from the time it left Dawson, the mail team arrived in Skagway. Buck and his team were worn out and worn down. His one hundred and forty pounds had dropped to one hundred and fifteen. The rest of the dogs had lost even more weight. Pike and Sol-leks limped along. Dub had a sore shoulder from pulling the sled. Every dog's feet hurt. They had no spring left in their steps but fell heavily on the trail with all their weight. This trudging along had made them even more tired.

It wasn't the kind of tired that comes with brief effort, which could be cured with a few hours' rest. It was the tiredness that comes through months of hard work that drains all of one's strength. Every muscle and cell was dead tired. And there was a reason for it. In less than five months they had gone twenty-five hundred miles. During the last eighteen hundred miles, they had rested for only five days. Now they were on their last legs.

Fresh batches of dogs were to take the places of those too worn out for the trail. Rather than take a break, the drivers were to sell the old team of tired dogs and move on.

"Mush on, poor sore feets," the driver told them as they went down the main street of town. "This is the last. Then we get one long rest, eh?"

The drivers thought they too would get a long rest. But many men had rushed into the Klondike, and many of their wives and girlfriends had not. So the mail was stacking up. Also, there were new orders. Fresh batches of dogs were to take the places of those too worn out for the trail. Rather than take a break, the drivers were to sell the old team of tired dogs and move on.

Three days passed. On the fourth day, two men from the States came along and bought them all cheaply. They called each other Hal and Charles. Charles was a middle-aged man with watery eyes and a mustache that he twisted up at the ends. Hal was a young man of nineteen or twenty with a gun and a hunting knife strapped on him. He wore a belt of **cartridges**[1] that made him seem immature and foolish. Both men were out of place in the North. Buck saw money pass between Charles and the government agent. He knew that the Scotch mailman and his drivers were passing out of his life, just as Perrault, François, and all the others had.

Buck and the other dogs went with their new owners to a sloppy camp. The tent was half up, the dishes unwashed, and things were lying around camp. A woman named Mercedes was there. She was Charles's wife and Hal's sister—a nice family party.

Buck watched them take down the tent and load the sled. They worked hard but not well. They rolled the tent into a bundle too large to fit on the

---

[1] **cartridges**—tubes of bullets.

sled. They packed the tin dishes unwashed. They put a sack of clothes on the front of the sled, but Mercedes said it should go in the back. When they had done so, and covered it up with other bundles, she said that she needed some of the clothes. So she made the men unload the sled to get at them. Three men from another tent came out and looked on. They smiled and winked at each other.

"You've got a big load as it is," said one of them. "I wouldn't take that tent along if I was you."

"Oh no!" cried Mercedes, throwing up her hands. "How in the world could I get along without a tent?"

"It's springtime. You won't get any more cold weather," the man told her.

She shook her head, so Charles and Hal put the last odds and ends on top of the huge load.

"Think it'll ride?" one of the men asked.

"Why shouldn't it?" Charles said angrily.

"Oh, that's all right," the man said. "I was just wondering. It seemed a bit top heavy."

Charles turned his back and drew the ropes tight.

"And you think the dogs can hike all day with that load behind them?" asked another man.

"Of course," said Hal. Then he swung his whip and shouted "Mush! Mush on there!"

The dogs leaned against the bands tied around their breasts. They strained hard for a few moments and then relaxed. They could not move the sled.

"The lazy brutes. I'll show them," Hal cried, drawing up his whip.

"The lazy brutes. I'll show them," Hal cried, drawing up his whip.

But Mercedes grabbed it from him. "The poor dears! You must promise you won't be harsh with them or I won't go one step."

"You don't know about dogs," her brother **sneered.**[2] "And I wish you'd leave me alone. You've got to whip them to make them go. That's their way. Ask anyone. Ask those men."

Mercedes looked at the men.

"They're weak as water, if you want to know," a man said. "They just need rest."

Hal cursed and Mercedes cried, "Oh!" Then she decided to stand up for her brother anyway.

---

[2] **sneered**—said with spite, scorn, or disrespect.

"Never mind that man," she said. "You're driving our dogs. You do what you think best with them."

Again Hal's whip fell upon the dogs. They pushed against the breast bands, dug their feet into the snow, and pulled with all their might. Still the sled held like an **anchor.**[3] After two tries, they stood panting. The whip sang out. Then Mercedes dropped to her knees by Buck. With tears in her eyes, she put her arms around his neck.

> **"You poor, poor dears," she cried. "Why don't you pull hard? Then you won't be whipped."**

"You poor, poor dears," she cried. "Why don't you pull hard? Then you won't be whipped." Buck did not like her, but he was feeling so unhappy, he did not resist her. He took it as part of the day's work.

One of the onlookers had been clenching his teeth.[4] Now he spoke up.

"It's not that I care what becomes of you. But for the dogs' sakes I just want to tell you, you can help them a lot by breaking that sled out from the

---

[3] **anchor**—a heavy metal object used to hold a ship or hot air balloon in place.

[4] clenching his teeth—an expression meaning to keep quiet so as not to show anger.

ice. The runners are frozen fast. Lean against your pole, right and left, and break the sled out."

A third time they tried, this time following the advice. The overloaded sled pushed ahead slowly. Buck and his mates struggled under Hal's whip. Soon the path turned and sloped steeply into the main street. Going downhill, Hal did not have the skills to keep the top-heavy sled from tipping over. As they all turned, it spilled half of its load. The dogs never stopped. They kept going as the sled, now light, slid behind them on its side. They were angry at how they had been treated. Buck was raging. He broke into a run, and the team followed. Hal cried "Whoa!", but they did not stop. The sled ran over him, and the dogs dashed on. Parts of the load lay all along the main street of town.

Kind people caught the dogs and picked up the belongings. Also, they gave advice—half the load and twice the dogs if the family ever wanted to reach Dawson. Hal and his brother-in-law began to listen.

They threw out the tent, all their canned foods, the tin dishes, and much of the clothing. Mercedes cried the whole time. She said she would not go on, even for a dozen husbands like Charles. But no one listened, so she finally wiped her eyes and started throwing things out.

They cut the load in half. Then Charles and Hal went out and bought six more dogs. This brought the team up to fourteen dogs. But the new dogs did not amount to much. They did not seem to know anything about the job. Buck could teach them what not to do, but he could not teach them what to do. They did not easily take to the trail.

> **But the new dogs did not amount to much. They did not seem to know anything about the job. Buck could teach them what not to do, but he could not teach them what to do.**

With the new dogs helpless and the old team worn out, the outlook was not good. Yet the two men were proud. They had never seen a sled with as many as fourteen dogs. There was a reason for that, of course. One sled could not carry the food of fourteen dogs. Charles and Hal did not yet know this. They had worked out the trip with a pencil to decide how much food to give each dog each day, and they thought their plan would work.

Late next morning Buck led the long team up the street. There was no snap or go in any of them.

They were starting out dead tired over the same path they had already run four times. Buck's heart was not in the work. The other dogs felt the same way. Buck could not depend on these two men and the woman. They did not know how to do anything. And it soon became clear that they could not learn. It took them half the night to pitch camp. It took half the morning to pack up and go. They loaded the sled so poorly that all day they had to stop and repack it. Some days they did not make ten miles. On other days they could not get started at all. Each day they figured out how much dog food to bring, and yet not once did they make it half as far as they had planned.

Buck could not depend on these two men and the woman. They did not know how to do anything.

Since the trip was taking so long, it was clear that they would be short on dog food. Still, they fed the dogs too much, using the food up even faster. The new dogs had not yet learned to make the most out of a little. And when the old dogs pulled weakly, Hal decided they needed more food. Sometimes

Mercedes stole food from the fish sacks and fed them even more. But all the dogs needed was rest. The heavy load robbed all their strength and slowed them down.

Then came the underfeeding. Hal awoke one day to the fact that his dog food was half gone. They had only covered one fourth of the miles they needed to go. He cut back on the dogs' food and tried to travel farther each day. But the dogs could not go any faster and the family could not get up any earlier, so the plan did not work well.

The newer dogs were not used to the lack of food. Sooner or later, all of them died.

The first to go was Dub, who had been a faithful worker. His sore shoulder went from bad to worse. With no treatment and no rest, he could not get better, so Hal shot him. The newer dogs were not used to the lack of food. Sooner or later, all of them died.

The family came to see that the arctic travel was too harsh for them. Mercedes stopped crying over the dogs and began crying for herself again. Then they all argued. They were never too **weary**[5] to argue. The patience of the trail, which comes to

---

[5] **weary**—tired, exhausted.

those who work hard and suffer and yet remain sweet and kind, did not come to these three. Their bones hurt, their heads ached, and their speech became cruel. They spoke hard words to each other from morning until night.

Charles and Hal each thought he did more than his share of the work. Mercedes sided first with one and then the other. So the quarrel never ended. As they argued, the fire went unbuilt, the camp unmade, and the dogs unfed.

Mercedes had become stiff and tired. She now took to riding on the sled. But her hundred and twenty pounds were too much for the weak animals. Charles and Hal begged her to get off and walk. All the while, she cried and called them brutes. They once tried to carry her off. They never did it again. She let her legs go limp and sat down on the trail. They went on their way, but she did not move. After they had gone three miles, they unloaded the sled, came back for her, and put her on the sled again.

Hal tried to harden everyone up, especially the dogs. He beat them with a club to make them tougher. Then when the dog food ran out, he traded his gun for a few pounds of frozen **horsehide**[6] to feed them. It tasted like iron. The dogs could not digest the hair nor draw any strength from the tough hide.

Through it all, Buck led the team as if in a bad dream. He pulled when he could. When he could no longer pull, he fell down and stayed there until blows from the whip or club drove him to his feet again. All the gloss went out of his furry coat. The hair hung limp or matted with dried blood where Hal's club beat him. He grew so thin that every rib showed. It was heartbreaking, but Buck's heart was unbreakable. The man in the red sweater had proved that.

As it was with Buck, so it was with his mates. The seven dogs all looked like bags of bones. They dropped as if dead every time the sled stopped. It always took the whip to get them up again. One day Billee finally fell and could not rise. Hal had traded away his gun and could not shoot Billee, so he hit him on the head with an ax handle and dragged his body off to the side. The next day another dog died. Only five dogs remained—Joe, Pike, Sol-leks, Teek, and Buck, who was blind with

---

[6] **horsehide**—the skin of a horse.

weakness and no longer asked much from the other dogs.

It was nice spring weather, but the dogs and humans did not care. Dawn came at three in the morning and it stayed light until nine at night. The winter silence gave way to the sounds of new life. The sounds came from things that had not moved during the long months of frost and now moved again. The **sap**[7] rose in the pines. The trees burst out in young buds. Crickets sang at night. In the day, all manner of creeping, crawling things came forth into the sun. Squirrels chattered, birds sang, and geese honked in clever wedges[8] that split the air.

From every hill came the sound of running water and the music of unseen fountains. All things were thawing, bending, snapping. The Yukon River was trying to break loose the ice that kept it down. It ate away from beneath, while the sun ate from above. Air holes formed. **Fissures**[9] sprang and spread apart. Chunks of thin ice fell into the river. And

---

[7] **sap**—fluid that runs through the tissues of plants.

[8] clever wedges—London refers to the geese flying together in the shape of a V.

[9] **fissures**—deep cracks.

amid all this awakening of life, under the blazing sun and through the soft-sighing breezes, came the two men, the woman, and the huskies.

With the dogs falling, Mercedes crying, Hal swearing, and Charles's eyes watering, they came into John Thornton's camp on the White River. When they halted, the dogs dropped down as if dead. Mercedes dried her eyes and looked at John Thornton. Charles sat down on a log to rest. Hal did the talking. John Thornton was **whittling**[10] an ax handle he had just made. He listened and gave advice when asked, though he knew they would not take the advice. He warned them not to take chances by crossing the river. The melting ice would break under the weight of the sled.

> **He warned them not to take chances by crossing the river. The melting ice would break under the weight of the sled.**

"They told us we couldn't make White River either, and here we are," Hal bragged.

"And they told you true," John Thornton said. "The bottom may drop out any time now. I tell you, I wouldn't cross that ice for all the gold in Alaska."

---

[10] **whittling**—carving wood with a knife.

"All the same, we'll go on to Dawson," Hal said. He raised his whip. "Get up there, Buck! Get up there! Mush on!"

Thornton went on whittling. He knew he could not keep fools from their **folly.**[11] But the team did not get up. The whip flashed out. John Thornton tightened his lips. Sol-leks crawled to his feet. Teek followed. Joe came next, yelping with pain. Pike tried three times before he could get up. Buck made no effort. He lay quietly where he had fallen. The lash bit into him again and again, but he did not whine or struggle. Thornton started to speak but changed his mind. Tears came into his eyes as the whipping went on and on.

This was the first time Buck had failed. That alone seemed reason enough for Hal's rage. He put down the whip and picked up the club. Buck still did not move under the rain of blows that now fell upon him. Like his mates, he was barely able to get up. But unlike them, he had made up his mind not to get up. He had a feeling of impending doom.[12]

---

[11] **folly**—foolish act or foolishness.

[12] a feeling of impending doom—a thought that something bad was about to happen.

He had felt the thin ice under his feet all day, and he knew it was not safe to cross the river. He had felt so much pain and gone so far that the blows did not hurt much any more. The spark of life in him was nearly out. Soon he could not feel anything. He seemed to watch the scene from a distance. He could hear the club hit his body. But it was no longer his body, it seemed so far away.

Suddenly he heard a cry that sounded like the cry of an animal. John Thornton sprang upon the man with the club. Hal fell backward. Mercedes screamed. Charles wiped his eyes but did not get up.

John Thornton stood over Buck, too angry to speak.

"If you strike that dog again, I'll kill you," he said at last.

"It's my dog," Hal told him, wiping blood from his mouth. "Get out of my way. I'm going to Dawson."

Thornton stood between Hal and Buck. He did not intend to get out of the way. Hal pulled out his hunting knife. Mercedes, **hysterical,**[13] yelled, cried, and laughed at once. Then Thornton struck Hal's hand with the ax handle, and the knife fell to the ground. He hit Hal's hand again as he tried to pick it up. Then he picked up the knife himself and cut Buck's traces.

Hal had no fight left in him. He had too many worries already. Besides, Buck was too near death to help haul the sled any more. A few minutes later they pulled out from the bank and down the river. Buck heard them go and raised his head to see. Pike was leading, Sol-leks was at the wheel, and between were Joe and Teek. They were limping along. Mercedes was riding the loaded sled. Hal guided and Charles was in the rear.

Besides, Buck was too near death to help haul the sled any more.

As Buck watched them, Thornton got down beside him and looked for broken bones. He found nothing but bruises and signs of starvation. By then the sled was a fourth of a mile away. Dog and man watched it crawl along the ice. Suddenly, they saw its back end drop down, as if in a **rut**.[14] Hal's pole jerked into the air as he clung to it. Mercedes

---

[13] **hysterical**—wildly emotional.

[14] **rut**—a deep track made by wheels in soft ground.

screamed. They saw Charles turn to run back. Then a whole chunk of ice gave way, and the dogs and humans were gone. A **yawning**[15] hole was all that was left of them. The bottom had dropped out of the trail.

John Thornton and Buck looked at each other.

"You poor thing," said John Thornton, and Buck licked his hand.

---

[15] **yawning**—wide open, gaping.

CHAPTER VI

For the Love of a Man

When John Thornton had frozen his feet earlier that year, his partners had left him to get well. They had gone on up the river to get a raft of logs so they could carry him to Dawson. He was still limping at the time he saved Buck, but as the days warmed up, the limp went away. And as Buck lay by the riverbank, looking at the water and listening to the songs of birds and the hum of nature, he also won back his strength.

Rest comes easy after one has walked three thousand miles. So Buck did not mind growing lazy as his wounds healed and his muscles swelled out. For that matter, they all loafed—Buck, John Thornton, and his dogs, Skeet and Nig. They waited for the raft to come and carry them down to Dawson. Skeet made friends with Buck from the start. She licked his wounds as a cat washes her kittens. He began to look forward to her doctoring. Nig, also friendly, was a large dog with eyes that laughed. To Buck's surprise, these dogs did not act jealous of him. They seemed to share the kindness of John Thornton. As Buck grew stronger, they taught him silly games. They even drew Thornton into the games. So Buck romped through his healing time into a new life. Pure love was his for the first time. This he had never had, even at Judge Miller's. He had worked as partners with the Judge's sons and grandsons. He had felt like a friend to the Judge. But it had taken John Thornton to stir this burning, adoring love.

He had felt like a friend to the Judge. But it had taken John Thornton to stir this burning, adoring love.

This man had saved his life. That was something, but there was more. He was the ideal master. Other men cared for their dogs out of duty. He cared for his dogs as if they were his own children, because he could not help it. He never forgot a kind greeting or a cheery word. He enjoyed sitting down for a long talk with the dogs. And he had a way of taking Buck's head between his hands, resting his own head upon Buck's, and shaking him back and forth. All the while he called Buck **profane**[1] names that to Buck were love names. Buck knew no greater joy than that rough embrace and name-calling. At each jerk it seemed that his heart would be shaken out of his body, so great was its joy. And when he sprang to his feet, his mouth laughed without making a sound and his eyes reached out to his master. Then John Thornton would say with awe, "You can almost speak!"

Buck had a trick for showing his love that almost caused pain. He would often grab Thornton's hand in his mouth. He would close it so tightly that his teeth left marks in the hand for some time. As Buck understood the name-calling to be love words, so the man took this bite for a caress.

Yet for the most part, Buck showed his love at a distance. He did not beg for love, even though he went wild with happiness when Thornton touched or spoke to him. Skeet would shove her nose under

---

[1] **profane**—vulgar, crude.

Thornton's hand until he petted her. Nig would rest his head on Thornton's legs. But Buck was happy just to lie at Thornton's feet for hours. He would look up into his face, study it, and watch his master's every move. Sometimes he would lie farther away and watch from behind. Then Buck's **gaze**[2] would draw John Thornton's head around and he would return the gaze without speech, his heart shining out of his eyes as Buck's heart shone out.

His many masters had left in him a fear that no master would stay for long. He was afraid that Thornton would pass out of his life as the others had.

For a long time after his rescue, Buck did not like Thornton to move out of his sight. From the moment he left the tent to when he came back, Buck would walk at his heels. His many masters had left in him a fear that no master would stay for long. He was afraid that Thornton would pass out of his life as the others had. Even at night, he dreamed about this fear. At such times, he would wake up and creep over to the flap of the tent. There he would stand and listen to the sound of his master's breathing.

---

[2] **gaze**—a steady look.

But in spite of his great love for John Thornton, he still had the wildness the Northland had bred in him. He was no longer stamped with the marks of a long line of city dogs. He was a thing of the wild, come in from the wild to sit by John Thornton's fire. Because of his great love, he could not steal from this man. Yet he could still slyly steal from any other man in any other camp.

These dogs soon knew that Buck could take their lives if he chose. And Buck had no mercy. He had learned well the law of club and fang.

Buck's face and body had the teeth marks of many dogs. He fought as fiercely as ever. Skeet and Nig would never argue with him, but he would fight dogs who were strangers. These dogs soon knew that Buck could take their lives if he chose. And Buck had no mercy. He had learned well the law of club and fang. He never drew back from a **foe**[3] he had started on the way to Death. He had learned from Spitz and from the fighting dogs of the police and mail carriers. He must master or be mastered. Mercy would only be taken for fear, and so it could lead to death. Kill or be killed, eat or be eaten, was the law. It had

---

[3] **foe**—enemy.

been passed down to him through time, and he obeyed it.

He was older than the days he had lived and the breaths he had taken. He linked the past with the present. The history of his species throbbed through him in a mighty rhythm, and he swayed to it as the tides and seasons sway. He sat by John Thornton's fire, a broad-breasted dog with white fangs and long fur. But behind him were the shades of all types of dogs and wolves. They were one with him, tasting the meat he ate, thirsting for the water he drank, and scenting the wind with him. They told him the sounds made by wild life in the forest. They gave him his moods and prompted his actions. They went to sleep with him, and they dreamed with him and became the stuff of his dreams.

So much did these forces call to him that each day the claims of man slipped farther from him. Deep in the forest, a call was sounding. As often as he heard this thrilling call, he felt the urge to turn his back on the fire and the beaten earth around it. Then he would plunge into the forest and run on and on. He knew not where or why, nor did he wonder. But as often as he ran out over the soft, unbroken earth into the green shade, his love for John Thornton always drew him back to the fire again.

Thornton alone held him. Other people meant nothing to Buck. Visitors might praise or pet him, but he was cold to them. He would walk away from a man too friendly. When Thornton's partners, Hans and Pete, arrived on the raft, Buck ignored them until he saw they were close to Thornton. After that, he took what they gave him, but only as a favor. He still did not warm up to them.

Yet for Thornton, Buck's love grew and grew. He alone could put a pack on Buck's back. Nothing was too great for Buck to do when Thornton asked.

Hans and Pete were like Thornton. They lived close to the earth, thinking simply and seeing clearly. They understood Buck and his ways, and they did not insist that he feel close to them. Yet for Thornton, Buck's love grew and grew. He alone could put a pack on Buck's back. Nothing was too great for Buck to do when Thornton asked.

One day the men and dogs were sitting on a cliff three hundred feet above a bed of rocks. John Thornton had a whim. To test Buck's loyalty, he waved his arm and said, "Jump, Buck!" The next thing he knew, he was holding Buck back from the edge of the cliff as Hans and Pete pulled them both to safety.

"It's amazing," Pete said after it was over.

Thornton shook his head. "It's good and it's awful too. Sometimes it scares me."

"I wouldn't want to be the man who lays hands on you while he's around," Pete said.

"Me neither," said Hans.

At Circle City, before the year was out, the thing Pete feared came to pass. "Black" Burton, an evil man, picked a fight with a younger man at the bar. Thornton stepped in between them. Buck was lying in a corner, head on paws, watching his master's every move. Then Burton struck out at Thornton, who fell against the rail of the bar.

Suddenly, those watching heard a great roar. They saw Buck's body rise up in the air and head for Burton's throat. The man threw out his arm to protect his throat, but he landed on the floor with Buck on top of him. Buck loosed his teeth from the man's arm and went for the throat again. This time he tore it open. Then the crowd was upon Buck. They pulled him off Burton and chased him away.

While a doctor checked the bleeding, Buck **prowled**[4] up and down, growling and trying to rush in again. Men with clubs had to chase him back.

The miners all met and decided the dog had good reason to attack, so they let him go. From that day on, his name spread through every camp in Alaska.

In the fall of that year, Buck saved John Thornton's life in another way. The three men were taking a long boat down a bad stretch of rapids.

In the fall of that year, Buck saved John Thornton's life in another way.

Hans and Pete ran along the bank. They held a rope tied to the boat, so it couldn't get away. Thornton stayed in the boat, pushing it the way it should go with a pole. Buck, on the bank, stayed close to the boat and kept his eyes on his master.

In one bad spot, a ledge of rocks jutted into the river. Hans threw some of the rope down the bank. He ran with the end in his hand, hoping to pull the boat along when it cleared the ledge. Thornton pushed off into the stream with his pole, but when the boat cleared the rocks, it got caught in the swift current and went flying downstream. Hans pulled the rope too suddenly. The boat went over and

---

[4] **prowled**—paced.

Thornton fell out. The current carried him downstream to the worst of the rapids. It was a stretch of wild water in which no swimmer could live.

Buck jumped in instantly. He swam through a mad swirl of water to reach Thornton and felt him grasp his tail. Then Buck headed for the bank, swimming with all his splendid strength. But they could not easily get to shore as the waves pushed them down the stream. From below came the deadly roaring where the wild current went wilder.

Buck jumped in instantly. He swam through a mad swirl of water to reach Thornton and felt him grasp his tail.

The river was torn into shreds and spray by the rocks, which stood like the teeth of a huge comb. The suck of the water was frightful. Thornton knew he could not get to shore. He scraped over one rock, then another. He hit the third rock with crushing force. He held onto its slick top with both hands, letting go of Buck. Above the roar of the churning water he shouted, "Go, Buck! Go!"

Buck could not hold his own. He was swept on downstream, trying but unable to get back. When he heard Thornton call out, he reared up out of the water for one last look. Then he obeyed, swimming powerfully to the bank. Pete and Hans dragged him ashore at the point where swimming became impossible.

They knew that the length of time a man could cling to a slippery rock was a matter of minutes, so they ran up to a point far above Thornton. Then they tied a rope to Buck's neck and shoulders and sent him into the stream. He swam out boldly but not straight enough into the stream. He soon started to slip past Thornton in the current. Hans pulled on the rope as though Buck were a boat. He was jerked under water and stayed there until his body hit the bank and he was half-drowned. Hans and Pete hauled him out. They pounded the breath into him and the water out of him. He tried to stand but fell down again. The faint sound of Thornton's voice came to them. They could not make out the words but knew he was in trouble. His master's voice acted on Buck like an electric shock. He jumped to his feet and ran up the bank to the point where he got in before.

Again they tied the rope to him and set him into the water. Again he swam out, but this time he went into the stream. He would not make the same mistake again. Hans let out the rope. Buck held on until he was straight upstream from Thornton. Then he turned and, with the speed of a train, headed down upon him. Thornton saw him coming. Buck struck him like a ram, with the force of the current behind him. As he did, Thornton reached up and closed both arms around the shaggy neck. Then Hans wrapped the rope around the tree, jerking Buck and Thornton under the water. Struggling, choking, and dragging over the jagged rocks, they veered toward the bank.

Thornton was badly bruised himself, but he rushed over to Buck and carefully looked over his body. The dog had three broken ribs.

Thornton came to, belly down and being rocked across a log by Hans and Pete. He looked around for Buck. Nig was starting to howl over Buck's limp body, while Skeet licked the wet face and closed eyes. Thornton was badly bruised himself, but he rushed over to Buck and carefully looked over his body. The dog had three broken ribs.

"We'll camp right here," Thornton said. And camp they did, until Buck's ribs healed and he was able to travel.

That winter at Dawson, Buck performed another **feat.**[5] This one put his name even higher on the totem-pole of Alaskan fame. It all began when some miners stood in a saloon talking about their best dogs. Thornton was there. They knew about Buck and began saying they doubted the stories they had heard about him. Thornton spoke up for Buck. Then one man stated that his dog could start and move a sled with five hundred pounds on it. Another one said six hundred for his dog. A third man said seven hundred.

"That's nothing!" said John Thornton. "Buck can start with a thousand pounds."

"And break it out of the ice? And walk with it for a hundred yards?" asked Matthewson, the man with the seven-hundred-pound claim.

"Yes," John Thornton said coolly.

"Well," Matthewson said in a loud voice. "I've got a thousand dollars that says he can't. And there it is." He slammed a sack of gold dust upon the bar.

Nobody spoke. Thornton's bluff had been called. He could feel himself blush. His tongue had tricked him. He did not know whether Buck could go with a thousand pounds. Half a ton! He had

---

[5] **feat**—amazing act.

great faith in Buck's strength, but never had he thought of really trying it, with a dozen men watching. Besides, he had no thousand dollars. Neither did Hans or Pete.

"I've got a sled outside now with twenty fifty-pound sacks of flour on it," Matthewson went on. "So don't let that stop you."

Thornton did not know what to say. He looked from face to face, hoping to find a friendly one. He finally saw the face of an old friend and whispered, "Can you lend me a thousand?"

"Sure," said the friend, thumping down his sack by Matthewson's. "Though I don't see how the beast can do the trick."

Everyone went out into the street to see the test. People made bets. Hundreds of men stood around the sled full of flour. It was sixty degrees below zero and the runners had frozen to the snow. Some of the men bet two-to-one that Buck could not move the sled. A question came up about whether Thornton would be allowed to knock the runners loose from the ice. Matthewson said that breaking out meant starting with the runners frozen in place. The men voted for Matthewson's way. Then the bets went three to one against Buck.

No one believed Buck could do the feat. Thornton now looked at the sled and its team of ten dogs. It seemed impossible, even to him, that Buck could pull the load out alone. Still, he wouldn't back down. The fighting spirit that soars above odds does not see the impossible. He called Hans and Pete to him. Together, the three men had only two hundred dollars. They bet it against Matthewson's six hundred dollars.

No one believed Buck could do the feat. Thornton now looked at the sled and its team of ten dogs. It seemed impossible, even to him, that Buck could pull the load out alone.

The team of ten dogs was unhitched, and Buck was put to the sled. He felt the excitement and knew that in some way he must do a great thing for John Thornton. The men stood and admired him. He was in perfect shape, one hundred and fifty pounds of grit. His furry coat shone like silk. The hair on his neck and shoulders seemed to lift with every movement. His broad breast, strong front legs, and full muscles shone. Men felt these muscles and called them hard as iron. The odds went back down to two to one.

"Sir!" said a rich miner. "I offer you eight hundred dollars for him before the test, just as he stands."

Thornton shook his head and stepped to Buck's side.

"You must stand off from him Thornton," Matthewson said. "Give him plenty of room."

The crowd fell silent except for the voices of gamblers urging others to take their bets. It was a hard sell. Everyone knew Buck was a strong animal, but twenty fifty-pound sacks of flour looked like too much weight, even for him.

"Do it out of love for me, Buck. Do it because you love me."

Thornton got down by Buck's side. He took Buck's head in his two hands and rested cheek on cheek. He did not shake Buck's head, as he would have, but whispered in his ear. "Do it out of love for me, Buck. Do it because you love me." Buck made a soft sound, holding back his eagerness. The crowd watched with wonder, as if the man and dog were working magic together. Then Thornton got to his feet. Buck took Thornton's hand between his jaws, pressing in with his teeth and slowly letting go. It was the answer of love Thornton had wanted. At last he stepped back.

"Now, Buck," he said.

Buck tightened the traces, then let them go a few inches. It was the way he had learned.

"Gee!" Thornton's voice rang out, sharp in the tense silence. The command meant to lean to the right. Buck swung to the right. The load jerked and the runners made a crisp sound as they broke from the ice.

"Haw!" Thornton yelled.

Buck did the same thing, but this time swung to the left. The ice snapped. The runners slid to the side. The sled was broken out.

"Now, MUSH!"

Thornton's call cracked out like a gunshot. Buck threw himself forward. His whole body was gathered up in the effort, the muscles growing like live things under the silky fur. His great chest and head were low to the ground. But his feet flew like mad, the claws digging and scraping into the snow. The sled swayed and almost started. One of his feet slipped, and one man groaned aloud. But he kept pulling. Then the sled moved ahead in a series of jerks. It never stopped again but went ahead half an inch, an inch, two inches. Finally, the jerks smoothed out and the sled picked up speed. Soon it was moving steadily along.

Men who had been holding their breath suddenly gasped and began to breathe again. Thornton ran behind, talking to Buck in short, cheery words. A pile of firewood marked the end of the hundred yards. As Buck neared it, a cheer began to grow and grow. It burst into a roar as he passed the firewood and halted at Thornton's command. Hats and mittens were flying in the air. Men were shaking hands and talking excitedly.

"Sir!" said the miner who wanted to buy Buck. "I'll give you a thousand for him, sir—no, twelve hundred, sir."

But Thornton fell on his knees beside Buck. Head was against head, and Thornton was shaking Buck's back and forth. Those who hurried up heard him calling Buck names, cursing him long and softly and lovingly.

"Sir!" said the miner who wanted to buy Buck. "I'll give you a thousand for him, sir—no, twelve hundred, sir."

Thornton rose to his feet. His eyes were wet. The tears ran down his cheeks. He turned to the man and said angrily, "No, sir. You can forget it. And don't ever ask again."

Buck took Thornton's hand in his teeth. Thornton shook him back and forth. As though by instinct, the onlookers drew back in respect. They did not interrupt again.

CHAPTER VII

The Sounding
of the Call

Buck had earned sixteen hundred dollars in five minutes for John Thornton. This made it possible for his master to pay off his debts and plan a trip. Thornton, Hans, and Pete wanted to go into the East to find a **fabled**[1] lost mine. The story of the mine was as old as the history of the country. Many men had looked for it, but few had found it. More than a few had never returned from the **quest**.[2] The story told of an old cabin next to a mine. The mine

---

[1] **fabled**—told of in legends, which may or may not be true.
[2] **quest**—the act of searching for something.

was full of gold **nuggets**[3] of a higher grade[4] than any others in the Northland. No one knew who had built the cabin or when or why.

No living man had **looted**[5] this treasure house, but many had died trying. Still, John Thornton, Pete, and Hans set out to look for it with Buck and half a dozen other dogs. They wanted to find what other men and dogs as good as they had failed to find. They sledded seventy miles up the Yukon River, then swung to the left into the Stewart River.

John Thornton asked little of man or nature. He was unafraid of the wild.

They followed it to the high peaks that marked the backbone of the North American continent.

John Thornton asked little of man or nature. He was unafraid of the wild. With a handful of salt and a rifle, he could head into the wilderness and stay as long as he pleased. He hunted his dinner as he traveled. If he failed to find his dinner, he kept going, like the Indian, knowing that sooner or later he would come to it. So on this great journey into the East, they took little but their tools and did not

---

[3] **nuggets**—lumps, usually of gold, or small pieces of something of great value.

[4] **higher grade**—higher quality; more pure.

[5] **looted**—stole from.

set a schedule. They looked ahead to a future without limits.

Buck felt endless joy hunting, fishing, and wandering through strange places. For weeks at a time they would camp here and there. The dogs **loafed.**[6] The men burned holes through the frozen mud and washed pans of dirt by the heat of the fire, looking for gold in the dirt. Sometimes they went hungry. Sometimes they feasted on **game.**[7] Summer came, and both dogs and men packed supplies on their backs to raft across blue lakes and float down rivers using logs as boats.

The months came and went. Back and forth they twisted through the **uncharted**[8] land, where no people were and yet where people had been if the Lost Cabin stories were true. They went across mountains in summer snowstorms. They shivered under the midnight sun[9] on naked mountains between the timber line[10] and the eternal snows.[11]

They dropped into summer valleys thick with bugs and flies. They picked perfect berries and

---

[6] **loafed**—relaxed, were lazy.

[7] **game**—wild animals or birds hunted by humans.

[8] **uncharted**—not surveyed; not noted on any map.

[9] midnight sun—the sun as it appears in summer in the far north. (It stays up almost all night in the summer, while it only appears for two to five hours each day in the winter.)

[10] timber line—the elevation above which it is too cold for trees to grow.

[11] eternal snows—snows that fall all year round, even in summer.

flowers in the shadows of glaciers. In the fall of the year, they went into a strange lake country. It was sad and silent with no signs of life. Chill winds blew, ice formed in the shade, and waves rippled on lonely beaches.

Through another winter they wandered, on the faded trails of men who had gone before. Once they came upon an **ancient**[12] path through the forest, and the Lost Cabin seemed very near. But the path began and ended nowhere, and the cabin remained a mystery. Another time they came upon an empty hunting lodge. John Thornton found an old trader's gun in some rotted blankets. But he found no sign of why the man left the gun and the lodge behind.

Spring came once more, but they still did not find the Lost Cabin. They did find a place in a broad valley where the gold showed like yellow butter across the bottom of the washing pan. They looked no more. Each day that they worked **panning**[13] this gold, they could earn thousands of dollars in gold dust and nuggets. So they worked every day. They put the gold in fifty-pound bags and piled them outside a lodge they made with spruce boughs.

---

[12] **ancient**—belonging to times long past.
[13] **panning**—washing gravel in a pan in search of gold.

Days flashed by like dreams as they piled up their treasure.

There was nothing for the dogs to do but haul in meat when Thornton hunted. So Buck spent long hours by the fire. The vision of the short-legged hairy man came to him more and more. The vision was just like the one he'd had before, when he worked for the Scotch mailman. Blinking by the fire, Buck wandered with the man in that other world that he remembered. What he remembered most was the man's fear. When the hairy man slept by the fire, he woke up often to peer into the darkness and throw more wood on the fire. When they walked on the beach, the hairy man found **shellfish**[14] and watched all around them as he ate. He seemed ready to run like the wind at the first sign of danger. They had sometimes crept quietly through the forest, with Buck at the hairy man's heels. Their ears and noses twitched, for the man heard and smelled as well as Buck. He could spring up into the trees or run fast on the ground. He could swing by his arms from limb to limb, letting go and catching. He never fell or missed his grip. In fact, he seemed as much at home in the trees as on the

---

[14] **shellfish**—water animals that have shells, such as oysters, clams, crabs, and shrimp.

ground. Buck remembered nights when the man slept in a tree while Buck kept watch below.

Buck not only had visions of the hairy man but also heard the call sounding in the depths of the forest. It filled him with unrest and desire. It left in him a sweet gladness. Sometimes when he heard the call, he went into the forest looking for it. He would thrust his nose into the cool wood moss or into the black soil where long grasses grew. He would snort with joy at the fat earth smells. Or he would crouch behind tree trunks, wide-eyed and wide-eared to all that moved about him. He did not know why he did these things. Perhaps he hoped to surprise this call when he found it.

Buck could not resist the urges that came to him. He would be lying in camp, dozing in the heat of the day, when suddenly his head would lift and his ears perk up. He would spring to his feet and dash away.

Buck could not resist the urges that came to him. He would be lying in camp, dozing in the heat of the day, when suddenly his head would lift and his ears perk up. He would spring to his feet and dash away. He would go on and on for hours through the forest and across the open spaces.

He loved to run down dry creek beds and to spy upon the birds in the woods. For a day at a time he would hide and watch the **partridges**[15] strut up and down. Most of all, he loved to run in the dim light of the summer midnights and listen to the sleeping forest. He read signs and sounds as a man may read a book, always looking for that strange something that called to him. And it called at all times for him to come.

One night he awoke with a start. From the forest came the call, or one note of it, for the call had many notes. This one was a long-drawn howl, like but unlike that of a husky dog. He knew he had heard it before. He sprang through the sleeping camp and dashed into the woods. As he came closer to the cry, he went more slowly. Finally he came to an open place among the trees. Looking out, he saw a long, lean timber wolf with nose pointed to the sky.

He made no noise, yet it stopped howling and sensed that he was there. Buck went into the open, half-crouching, his tail stiff. Every movement held

---

[15] **partridges**—plump, brown game birds.

threat as well as friendliness. It was the **truce**[16] that marks the meeting of wild beasts that **prey.**[17] But the wolf ran at the sight of him. He followed the wolf, leaping to catch up. They ran in the bed of the creek, but a log jam blocked the path. The wolf whirled about, standing on its hind legs, snarling and snapping its teeth together.

Buck did not attack. He circled the wolf and made the signs of friendship. The wolf was afraid, for Buck was three times larger than he was.

Buck did not attack. He circled the wolf and made the signs of friendship. The wolf was afraid, for Buck was three times larger than he was. He got a chance to dart away, and the chase went on. Time and again Buck cornered him. He was in poor condition or Buck could not have overtaken him.

But in the end Buck's **persistence**[18] paid off, for the wolf finally saw that he meant no harm. The wolf sniffed noses with him. Then they became friendly and played about in the nervous way fierce beasts will do. After some time, the wolf

---

[16] **truce**—an agreement not to fight for the time being.

[17] **prey** (pronounced pray)—to kill and eat other animals.

[18] **persistence**—ability to stand firm; stubbornness.

loped[19] away. He made it clear to Buck that he was to come along. They ran side by side through the twilight. They went up the creek bed, into the **gorge**[20] from which it came, and across the **divide**[21] where it rose.

On the opposite slope of the **watershed,**[22] they came down onto flat land. They saw long stretches of forest cut by many streams. They ran through the woods hour after hour, as the sun rose higher and the day grew warmer. Buck was wildly glad. He knew he was at last answering the call. He was running by the side of his wood brother, going to the place from where the call came. Old memories were coming upon him fast. He had done this thing before, somewhere in that other world, and he was doing it again now. He was running free in the open, the **unpacked**[23] earth underfoot, the wide sky overhead.

They stopped by a running stream to drink. Suddenly, Buck remembered John Thornton. He sat down. The wolf started on toward the place from where the call surely came. When he saw Buck

---

[19] **loped**—ran with long strides.

[20] **gorge**—a narrow, steep-sided valley.

[21] **divide**—high land where the streams on one side flow into one river and the streams on the other side flow into another river.

[22] **watershed**—another word for a divide.

[23] **unpacked**—not walked on; not packed down into a path by the weight of animal or human feet.

sitting, he came back and sniffed noses, as though telling him to come. But Buck turned and headed slowly back. For most of an hour, the wild brother ran at his side, whining softly. Then he sat down, pointed his nose up, and howled. It was a mournful howl. As Buck kept going, he heard it grow faint and fainter until he could hear it no more.

But after two days, the call in the forest began to sound more insistently than before. Buck grew restless again.

John Thornton was eating dinner when Buck dashed into camp. He jumped upon his master in a wild show of love. He licked his face and bit his hand as John Thornton rocked him back and forth and cursed him lovingly.

For two days and nights, Buck never left camp. He never let Thornton out of his sight. He followed him as he worked, watched him while he ate, saw him into his bed at night and out of it in the morning. But after two days, the call in the forest began to sound more insistently than before. Buck grew restless again. He was haunted by the thought of the wild brother, the smiling land beyond the divide, and the long run through the forest. Once again he took to wandering in the woods. But the wild brother came no more, and though he listened long and hard, the howl was never raised.

He began to sleep out at night. He stayed away from camp for days at a time. Once he crossed the divide and went into the land of timber and streams. There he stayed for a week, looking for signs of the wild brother. He killed his meat as he went. He ran with an easy lope that seemed never to tire. He fished in a big stream. By this stream he killed a large black bear. Mosquitoes had blinded the bear as it fished. Now it went raging through the forest, helpless and angry. Even so, it was a hard fight. Two days later, he returned to his kill and had to chase off a dozen **wolverines,**[24] who had come to eat the leftovers. He killed two of them, and the others ran away.

The longing for blood became stronger than ever before. Buck was a killer, a thing that preyed. He lived on the things that lived, staying alive by showing his own strength in a world where only the strong survived. Because of all this, he took great pride in himself. It showed in the way he moved, walked, flexed his muscles, and showed off

---

[24] **wolverines**—small animals related to weasels.

his furry coat. If it weren't for the brown on his **muzzle**[25] and the splash of white hair that ran down his chest, he would have looked like a huge wolf, larger than any other. His St. Bernard father had given him his size, but he had the shape of his shepherd mother. His muzzle was the long wolf muzzle. His head looked like a very broad wolf head.

His cunning was wolf cunning and wild cunning. Yet he was smart as a St. Bernard or a shepherd. He had all of this, plus the lessons learned in the rugged North. It made him as fearsome an animal as any that roamed the wild. He lived on a diet of meat, which gave him even greater strength. Every part of him—brain, body, nerve and fiber—worked together perfectly. He leaped as fast as lightning to sights, sounds, and events that called for action. He could move twice as fast as a husky dog. He could act in the time it took for another dog to see the need to act. He seemed to see, think, and respond in the same moment. His muscles worked like steel springs. Life streamed through him in a flood, as if it would burst and pour out over the world.

---

[25] **muzzle**—the projecting nose and mouth of some animals, such as dogs and wolves.

"Never was there such a dog," said John Thornton one day, as his partners watched Buck marching out of camp.

"When he was made, the mold was broke,"[26] said Pete.

"By jingo! I think so myself," Hans agreed.

They saw him marching out of camp, but they did not see the change that took place as soon as he was hidden in the forest. He no longer marched. At once he became a thing of the wild, sneaking along softly, cat-footed, in the shadows. He knew how to stay under cover, to crawl on his belly like a snake, and to leap and strike like a snake. He could take a bird from its nest, kill a rabbit as it slept, and snap in mid-air the chipmunks running for the trees. Fish in open pools were not too quick for him. Beavers were not too careful for him to catch them. He killed to eat, not without reason, but he liked to eat only what he had killed himself. So when he was not hungry, sometimes he teased

He killed to eat, not without reason, but he liked to eat only what he had killed himself.

---

[26] the mold was broke (broken)—an expression meaning that one was born with abnormal and superior qualities, and that one stands out among his peers.

his victims. He would chase squirrels and then, when he had them, let them go.

As the fall of the year came on, the moose moved down into the lower valleys. Buck had already killed a stray calf, but he wanted to catch a larger moose. One day, he found a band of twenty. The chief bull moose was fierce and big. He stood more than six feet from the ground. This was as great a foe as Buck could ever want. He had antlers with fourteen points that spread seven feet across, from tip to tip. He waved the antlers back and forth, and his small eyes burned with a bitter light. He roared with fury at the sight of Buck.

The end of a feathered arrow stuck out of the bull's side. This explained his great anger. Guided by that instinct which came from the hunting days of old, Buck started to chase the bull away from the herd. It was no easy job. He barked and danced in front of the bull. He stayed just out of reach of the antlers and hoofs, which could have stamped out his life with one blow. The bull could not turn his back on the dog, which made him full of rage. He charged Buck, who jumped back, pretending he could not escape, so the bull would come closer.

When he got the bull away from the herd, two or three of the younger bulls would charge back upon Buck and let the wounded bull get back to the herd.

Saving this one member of the herd slowed them down. Losing him would not hurt the life of the herd.

There is a patience of the wild, tireless as life itself. This patience lets the spider stand for hours in its web. It lets the snake stay still in its coils. It helps the panther not to move in its hiding place. This patience belonged to Buck as he clung to the herd, slowing its march, worrying the mother cows, and driving the old bull mad. For half a day this went on. Buck attacked from all sides. He drove out his victim as fast as it could get back to its mates. Buck wore out his prey. He was the hunter, and he had more patience than the animals he hunted.

The day wore on and the sun dropped. The young bulls grew tired of going back to rescue their leader. Winter was rushing them in their journey to the lower valleys, and they were losing time. Saving this one member of the herd slowed them down. Losing him would not hurt the life of the herd. In the end, they left him behind, for the good of the herd.

As night fell, the old bull watched his mates move quickly away in the fading light. The cows he had known, the calves he had fathered, the bulls he had taught all slipped away. He could not follow, for the **fanged**[27] terror still leaped before his nose. The bull weighed eight hundred pounds. He had lived a long, strong life, full of fight. At the end, he faced death at the teeth of a dog whose head only reached his knees.

From then on, night and day, Buck never left his **prey.**[28] He did not let the bull moose look for food among the trees. He did not let him drink water in the streams they crossed. When the bull tried to run, Buck followed behind, lying down when the moose stopped and attacking him when he tried to eat or drink. The big head drooped under its tree of horns. The trot grew weaker and weaker. The bull would stand for a long time with its nose to the ground and its ears dropped. Then Buck would go get a drink of water and get some rest.

Buck noted a change in the air. He knew it not by sight, sound, or smell but by some other sense.

---

[27] **fanged**—having long, sharp teeth.

[28] **prey**—the noun form of prey, meaning the animal preyed upon.

He knew that strange things were coming. Yet he had to finish what he had started before he could explore the change.

At the end of the fourth day, he pulled the great moose down. For a day and a night he stayed by his kill, eating and sleeping. Then, feeling rested and strong, he turned his face toward camp and John Thornton. He loped for hours, never losing his way home. He crossed through strange country more surely than a **compass**[29] can point the way to go.

At the end of the fourth day, he pulled the great moose down. For a day and a night he stayed by his kill, eating and sleeping.

As he went, he became more aware of the new stir in the land. The wildlife differed from the life that had been there during the summer. The birds and squirrels talked of it and the breeze spoke of it. He stopped and sniffed the morning air, reading a message that made him leap on with greater speed. He came to know that something awful had taken place. He crossed the watershed, dropped down into the valley, and walked warily toward camp.

---

[29] **compass**—a device with a magnetic needle that always points north, used to keep people from getting lost.

Three miles away, he came upon a fresh trail that made his neck hair stand up. The trail led toward camp and John Thornton. Buck hurried on swiftly, every nerve straining. He noticed that almost all the birds and squirrels had fled. He smelled the scent of strangers on the trail. Then his nose jerked to the side. The new scent led him into some bushes where Nig was lying on his side. He lay dead with an arrow through his body.

A hundred yards farther on, Buck saw one of the sled dogs Thornton had bought in Dawson. This dog was thrashing around, almost dead. Buck passed him without stopping. From the camp came the sound of many voices, rising and falling in a sing-song chant. Creeping to the edge of the clearing, he found Hans lying on his face. He was covered with arrows like a **porcupine.**[30] At the same time, Buck looked out where the spruce-bough lodge had been. What he saw made his hair leap up on his neck and shoulders. A gust of rage swept over him. He did not know that he growled, but he growled loudly. Then, for the last time in his life, he acted out of **passion**[31]

---

[30] **porcupine**—a rodent with a body and tail covered with spines.

[31] **passion**—strong feelings or beliefs.

more than **reason.**[32] Because of his great love for John Thornton, he lost his head.

The Yeehats Indians were dancing around the ruined lodge when they heard a fearful roaring.

The Yeehats Indians were dancing around the ruined lodge when they heard a fearful roaring. They saw rushing upon them an animal like none they had ever seen before. It was Buck, a live hurricane of fury, hurling himself upon them. He had come to destroy. He sprang at the chief of the Yeehats, ripping the throat wide open until it spurted blood. He did not pause but leaped upon another man, tearing another throat open. There was no stopping him. He plunged about, tearing, destroying, and moving so quickly that their arrows could not hit him. In fact, the Indians were so close together that when they aimed at him, they hit each other. One young hunter, hurling a spear at Buck, drove it through the chest of another hunter. It landed with such force that the point went through the man's body and stuck out of his back. In a panic, the Yeehats ran off into the woods. They thought they were fleeing the Evil Spirit.

Truly Buck was like an evil force, raging at their heels and dragging them down like deer. It was a sad

---

[32] **reason**—the act of thinking and using logic.

day for the Yeehats. They scattered far and wide. It took them a week to find each other and count their losses. But Buck tired of chasing them and returned to the empty camp. He found Pete where he had been killed in his blankets. Buck could smell Thornton's scent in the earth, and he knew that his master had struggled. Thornton's struggle had ended in a deep pool. The water was muddy, but Buck followed the scent until he found Thornton's body hidden under water. At the edge of the pool, Skeet lay half in the water.

> *Buck could smell Thornton's scent in the earth, and he knew that his master had struggled. Thornton's struggle had ended in a deep pool.*

All day Buck brooded by the pool or walked restlessly around the camp. He understood death as an end of movement and a passing away from the lives of the living. And he knew John Thornton was dead. It left a great hunger in him, which ached and ached, and which food could not fill. At times, when he looked at the bodies of the Yeehats, he forgot his pain and felt pride in his kill. For he had killed man, the hardest game to kill. And he had done it in the face of the law of club and fang.[33]

---

[33] in the face of the law of club and fang—even though the men had weapons, which normally made them the killers.

He sniffed the Yeehats' bodies. They had died so easily. It was harder to kill a husky dog than to kill them. They would have been no match at all, were it not for their arrows and spears and clubs. After that, he would not be afraid of men except when they held their arrows, spears, and clubs.

Night came on. A full moon rose high over the trees. The light bathed the land until it almost looked like day. Brooding by the pool, Buck felt the stirring of the new life in the forest. He stood up, listening and scenting. From far away came a faint, sharp yelp. A chorus of yelps followed. The yelps grew closer and louder. Again Buck knew them as things heard in that other world that he still remembered. He walked to the center of the open space and listened. It was the call, the many-noted call. Now it **lured**[34] him more than ever before. And as never before, he was ready to obey. John Thornton was dead. The last tie

> *It was the call, the many-noted call. Now it lured him more than ever before. And as never before, he was ready to obey. John Thornton was dead. The last tie was broken.*

---

[34] **lured**—attracted one strongly.

was broken. Man and the claims of men no longer held him.

The wolf pack had at last crossed over from the land of streams and timber. They hunted the moose, as the Yeehats did, so they had followed the herd into Buck's valley. They poured into the moonlit clearing. In the center of the clearing, Buck stood like a statue, waiting for their coming. They were awed by how still and large he stood. After a moment's pause, the boldest one leaped for Buck. Like a flash Buck struck, breaking the wolf's neck. Then he stood, not moving, as the wolf rolled in pain. Three others tried it. One after the other, they drew back, bleeding from the throat or shoulder.

They poured into the moonlit clearing. In the center of the clearing, Buck stood like a statue, waiting for their coming.

This was enough. The whole pack came forward, crowded together, trying to pull down the prey. But Buck's quickness came into play. Turning on his back legs, snapping and gashing, he was everywhere at once. He whirled so quickly that no one could hurt him. To keep them from getting behind him, he stepped back into the creek bed. He stood before a high gravel wall the men had made. Now he had walls on three sides. He only had to face the front. So well did he face it that at the end of half an hour, the wolves drew back. Their tongues hung out. Their white fangs looked cruel and white in the moonlight. Some were lying down. Others stood watching him. Still others lapped water from the pool. One wolf, long and lean and gray, slowly came to him in a friendly way. Buck knew he was the wild brother he had run with for a night and a day. The brother whined softly. As Buck whined, they touched noses.

Then an old wolf came forward. Buck got ready to snarl but sniffed noses with him. Then the old wolf sat down, pointed his nose at the moon, and broke out in a long wolf howl. The others sat down and howled. And now the call came to Buck. He, too, sat down and howled. This over, he came out of his corner and the pack crowded around him sniffing. The leaders howled the yelp of the pack and ran away into the woods. The wolves fell in behind, yelping together. Buck ran with them, side by side with the wild brother. He yelped as he ran.

Buck ran with them, side by side with the wild brother.

And here may well end the story of Buck. In the years to come, the Yeehats noted a change in the breed of timber wolves. Some had splashes of brown on head and muzzle. Some had white marks on their chests. The Yeehats also tell of a Ghost Dog that runs at the head of the pack. They are afraid of this Ghost Dog, for it is smarter then they are. It steals from their camps, robs their traps, kills their dogs, and escapes their bravest hunters.

The tale grows worse. Some hunters fail to return to the camp. Some hunters are found with throats slashed open and wolf prints around them, larger than the prints of any wolf. Each fall, when the Yeehats follow the trail of the moose, there is one valley they never enter. They tell sad stories of how the Evil Spirit came to live in that valley.

The Yeehats do not know that in the summers, something does visit that valley. It is a great wolf with a beautiful coat. He is like and yet unlike all other wolves. The wolf crosses alone from the smiling timber land and comes down into an open space among the trees. Here a yellow stream flows from rotted moose-hide sacks and sinks into the ground. Long grass grows through it and hides its yellow from the sun. Here the wolf comes to lie and dream for awhile. He howls once, long and sadly, before he leaves.

But he is not always alone. When the long winter nights come on and the wolves follow their meat into the lower valleys, he stays at the head of the pack. They come through the pale moonlight and run beneath the northern lights. He leaps above his mates, his great throat full as he sings a song of the younger world,[35] which is the song of the pack.

---

[35] younger world—the world in earlier times, when wildness ruled.